Jungle Law

By Jill Eggleton

Illustrated by Serena Kearns

Jungle Law

Dr. Ronco was a scientist who spent months in the jungle studying animal and plant life. This is a recount of an event during that time . . .

JUNE 12
- It's hot & damp
- and the food
- tastes like insects.
- And that really bugs me.

JUNE 18
- The Monkeys seer to love my bananas.
- The proble
- so do

It was July 6. Dr. Ronco had been in the jungle for six weeks. He had become used to the smell of damp, decaying leaves. He had become used to the noises of insects and birds and other jungle animals. He had even become used to the heat and the rain and the clouds that suddenly formed and floated like ghosts among the trees and vines. He had eaten jungle nuts and berries. He had eaten bugs and beetles and caterpillar soup.

In his book, *How to Survive in the Jungle*, he had discovered that he could eat ants if he cooked them. He learned that ants were a good, nourishing snack. Dr. Ronco had learned, too, how to make his own night shelter. He always made it high up off the ground and away from the river, in case of flooding.

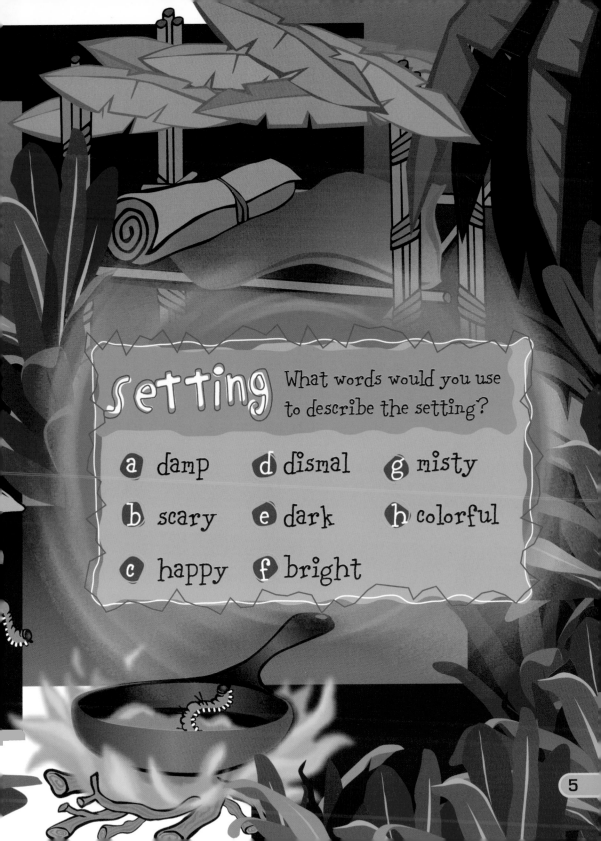

setting What words would you use to describe the setting?

a damp   d dismal   g misty

b scary   e dark   h colorful

c happy   f bright

On this trip, he had seen huge, hairy tarantulas and scorpions with stingers in their tails. He had seen crocodiles and flesh-eating piranhas. He had watched a boa constrictor squeeze its prey and swallow it whole. Dr. Ronco didn't like it, but he knew that was the law of the jungle.

But among the animals that interested Dr. Ronco the most was the jaguar. This beautiful, sleek creature was a clever and cunning hunter. It could stalk and swim and climb. It seemed to be always watching, waiting to pounce. It was the biggest predator in the jungle. But the jaguar faced danger of extinction if jungles continued to be destroyed. Dr. Ronco studied the jaguar from a distance.

Inference:

Dr. Ronco studied the jaguar from a distance ...

What inference can be made about how safe Dr. Ronco felt?

Fact or Opinion:

This beautiful, sleek creature was a clever and cunning hunter.

Fact or Opinion?

Fact – A statement that can be proved to be true

Opinion – A view or belief that is not based on fact or knowledge

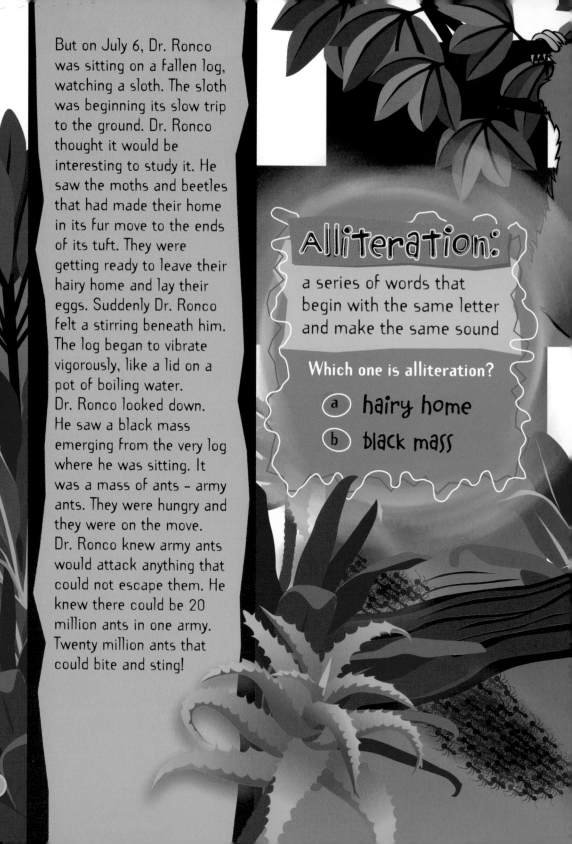

But on July 6, Dr. Ronco was sitting on a fallen log, watching a sloth. The sloth was beginning its slow trip to the ground. Dr. Ronco thought it would be interesting to study it. He saw the moths and beetles that had made their home in its fur move to the ends of its tuft. They were getting ready to leave their hairy home and lay their eggs. Suddenly Dr. Ronco felt a stirring beneath him. The log began to vibrate vigorously, like a lid on a pot of boiling water. Dr. Ronco looked down. He saw a black mass emerging from the very log where he was sitting. It was a mass of ants – army ants. They were hungry and they were on the move. Dr. Ronco knew army ants would attack anything that could not escape them. He knew there could be 20 million ants in one army. Twenty million ants that could bite and sting!

Alliteration:

a series of words that begin with the same letter and make the same sound

Which one is alliteration?

a hairy home

b black mass

Dr. Ronco started to run, but some ants had already locked themselves to his ankles.

Even through his thick socks, Dr. Ronco felt the piercing stings, like the stinging thorns of a cactus. The words in his book, *How to Survive in the Jungle*, leaped off the page and danced before his eyes. *Knock them off, scatter them. Without each other they are helpless. Knock them off, scatter them. Without each other they are helpless.*

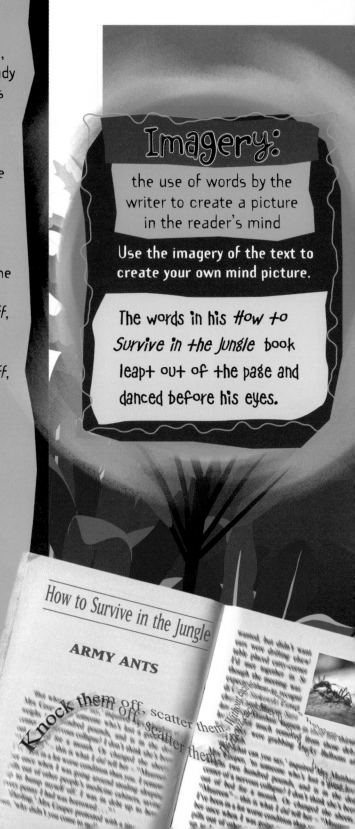

Imagery:

the use of words by the writer to create a picture in the reader's mind

Use the imagery of the text to create your own mind picture.

The words in his *How to Survive in the Jungle* book leapt out of the page and danced before his eyes.

How to Survive in the Jungle

ARMY ANTS

Knock them off, scatter them. Without each other they are helpless. Knock them off, scatter them. Without each other they are helpless.

44

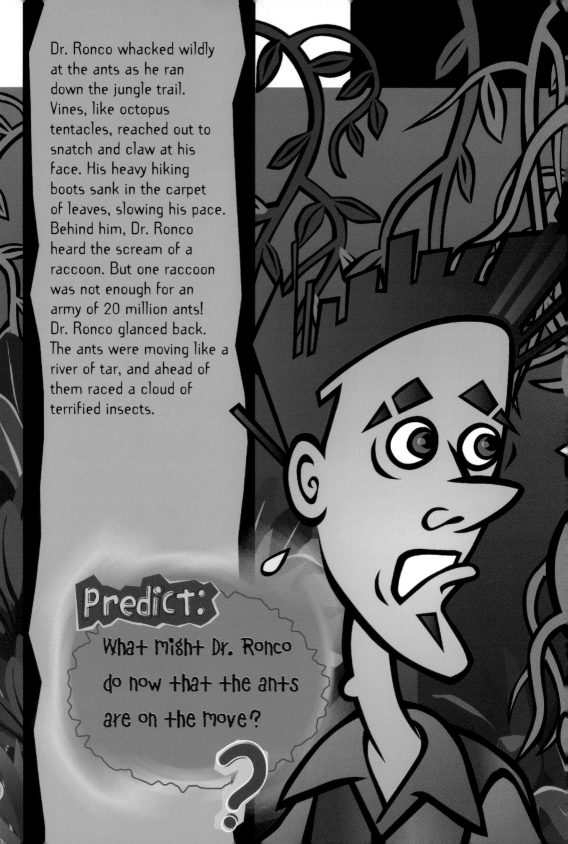

Dr. Ronco whacked wildly at the ants as he ran down the jungle trail. Vines, like octopus tentacles, reached out to snatch and claw at his face. His heavy hiking boots sank in the carpet of leaves, slowing his pace. Behind him, Dr. Ronco heard the scream of a raccoon. But one raccoon was not enough for an army of 20 million ants! Dr. Ronco glanced back. The ants were moving like a river of tar, and ahead of them raced a cloud of terrified insects.

Predict:

What might Dr. Ronco do now that the ants are on the move?

A simile compares one thing to another by using the word "like" or "as," and often creates a mental picture in the reader's mind.

A metaphor compares one thing to another without using the word "like" or "as," and often creates a mental picture in the reader's mind.

Metaphor or simile?

Vines like octopus tentacles

A cloud of terrified insects

Which is the metaphor?

Dr. Ronco scrambled across a gully, but the ants followed. They made an ant bridge – ants holding onto ants, holding onto ants. Dr. Ronco saw a lake. He could dive in there – the ants would not follow him into a lake. But he remembered the piranhas. This lake was probably their home. So he grabbed hold of a vine that dangled from a tree and swung himself into the branches.

clarify:
Gully

A a small valley

B canyon

C cliff

A, B, or C ?

Inference:

What inference can you make about Dr. Ronco's character?

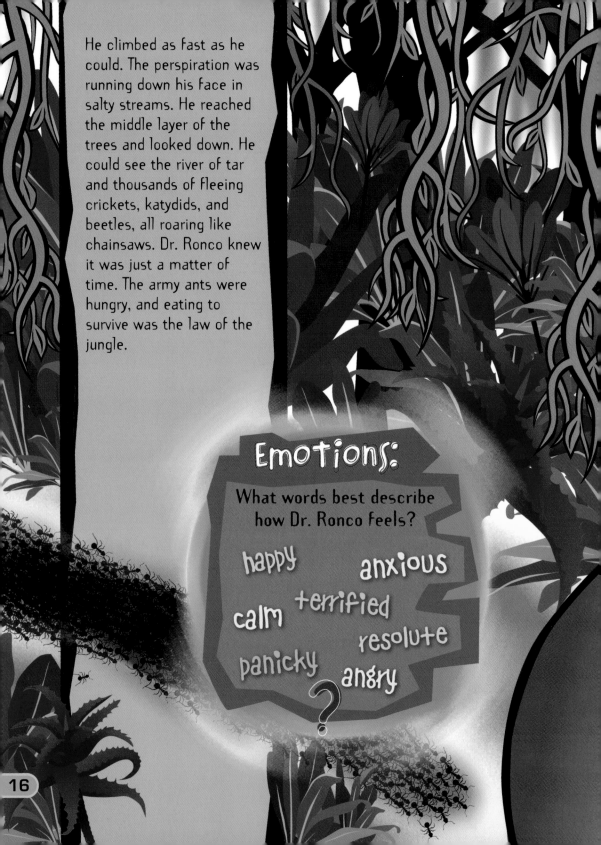

He climbed as fast as he could. The perspiration was running down his face in salty streams. He reached the middle layer of the trees and looked down. He could see the river of tar and thousands of fleeing crickets, katydids, and beetles, all roaring like chainsaws. Dr. Ronco knew it was just a matter of time. The army ants were hungry, and eating to survive was the law of the jungle.

Emotions:

What words best describe how Dr. Ronco feels?

happy

anxious

calm

terrified

resolute

panicky

angry

?

metaphor or simile:

See page 13 before you
make up your mind.

... roaring like chainsaws.

Is this a metaphor or simile?

Then Dr. Ronco saw the jaguar. It was lying stretched out in a patch of dappled sunlight. It was sleeping. It hadn't heard the army ants.

clarify:

Dappled

- Ⓐ hidden
- Ⓑ broken-up, mottled
- Ⓒ bright

A, B, or C?

Predict:

What do you think could happen in the story now?

19

Dr. Ronco knew that 20 million army ants could easily devour the jaguar. He climbed down the tree a little. He could see the river of tar surging closer. He had to alert the jaguar. He grabbed some berries off the tree and threw them, hard . . . onto the sleeping jaguar. The berries peppered the jaguar's sleek back. They burst, leaving red, blood-like stains on its silky fur.

The jaguar woke with a start. The words in the book, *How to Survive in the Jungle*, danced before Dr. Ronco's eyes again. *Don't tease or frighten animals. Treat them with respect.*

The jaguar leaped up. It crouched, ready to spring, an angry, menacing look in its eyes. The river of tar was surging closer. Dr. Ronco climbed up higher into the tree. He thought the jaguar might leap into the tree at any moment. He imagined its claws slicing him like a carving knife. But the jaguar had seen the army ants. It fled down the jungle trail.

synonym:

A word or phrase with a similar meaning to another word or phrase

Which word is the synonym for menacing?

A annoyed

B hungry

C threatening

A, B, or C ?

It was some time before Dr. Ronco could climb down from the tree. The sight of a poison-arrow frog sitting on a nearby limb propelled him. The army ants – that black river of tar – had moved on. But they had left their mark – empty skeletons littered the jungle trail.

Clarify:

Propelled

A drove or caused to move

B unseated

C turned

A, B, or C ?

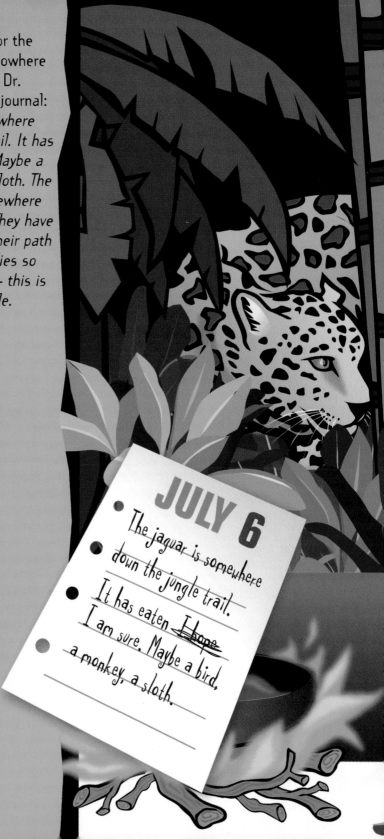

Dr. Ronco looked for the jaguar, but it was nowhere in sight. That night, Dr. Ronco wrote in his journal: *The jaguar is somewhere down the jungle trail. It has eaten, I am sure. Maybe a bird, a monkey, a sloth. The army ants are somewhere in a new bivouac. They have eaten. Nothing in their path has survived. One dies so another might live – this is the law of the jungle.*

JUL

- The army ants
- somewhere in a new bivouac. They have eaten. Nothing in their path has survived. One

JULY

- The army ants
- somewhere bivouac.

JULY 6

- The jaguar is somewhere down the jungle trail.
- It has eaten. ~~I hope~~ I am sure. Maybe a bird, a monkey, a sloth.

Summary:

- Dr. Ronco studies the jaguar in the jungle.
- Dr. Ronco studies the sloth.
- He sees the army ants are on the move.
- He flees the invading ants.
- He sees the jaguar sleeping in the sun, unaware of the ants.
- Dr. Ronco flees across a gully.
- He throws berries at the jaguar to wake it up.
- The jaguar flees.
- Dr. Ronco sees all the skeletons lying around in the jungle.
- Dr. Ronco knows the jaguar is safe and has to search for it again.

Select the main points you would include in a summary of *Jungle Law*.

Think About the Text

Making connections — What connections can you make to the text?

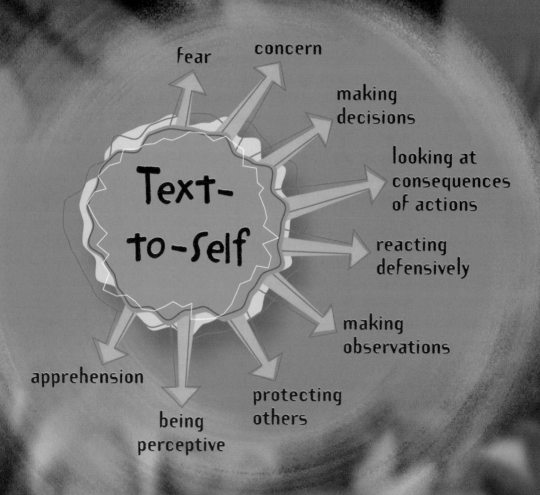

fear

concern

making decisions

looking at consequences of actions

reacting defensively

Text-to-Self

making observations

reacting defensively

apprehension

being perceptive

protecting others

Text-to-Text

Talk about other stories you may have read that have similar features. Compare the stories.

Text-to-World

Talk about situations in the world that might connect to elements in the story.

Planning a factual Recount

① Select a real event or experience.

② Make a plan.
Think about:

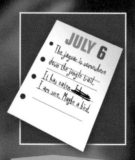

Who

When

Where

What